Once Upon A Time

Once Upon A Time

A Financial Fable

Carl Andersen

Illustrated by Alba Escayo
Edited and designed by Erin Long of Biblio/Tech

Dedication

This book is dedicated to the Founding Members of the Gold Is Money Internet Forum:

G-Khan, Barnacle Bob, Scorpio, Torus, skyvike, Au- Myn, Silver Streak, and Founding Fathers. Also to gpond who, although not formally a founder, put more heart and more work into the website than most of the real founders and who also turned out to be a great friend. And to the current stewards of Gold is Money, Scorpio, TnAndy, AgAuGal, and RichG: Thanks for keeping the spirit alive.

All the discussion, debates, and education over the years about honest money, precious metals, and many other important subjects have had a profound influence on my life.

Carl M. Andersen

Once upon a time, there was a powerful Island Kingdom with a strong navy and colonies far and wide. A king and a queen ruled the island, and the colonies, and all their royal subjects.

Some of the royal subjects were unhappy because the king tried to force them to believe in his god instead of the god they wanted to believe in. Also, it was very difficult for a poor person to earn money, to care for a family, or to buy a house. They felt like slaves to the king because of his control of their lives, forced religion, and very heavy taxes. Some of these unhappy people, the Freedomlovers, heard about a place where there was no king, only beautiful beaches, great forests, and huge mountains. A lovely place where the people could choose their own god and would be free to do whatever they wished with their lives. The Freedomlovers did not want to be anyone's slave, not even a king's slave. This belief in freedom from slavery was so strong that their great-great-great-grandchildren fought among themselves in a bloody and terrible war to end slavery forever in their new land, but that is another story for another time.

So these brave people packed up their families and their things and left their homes behind to find a new life in this new place. They pooled their little bit of money to hire a small ship, the Aprilflower, and its brave captain, Smit Johnson, to take them to what

they now called "Opportunityland." Since only one or two ships that they knew of had ever made the trip, no one (not even the captain) was quite sure how to get there. All they really knew was that they wanted to go there very badly.

Well, the people were eager and their captain was brave, so they left their home and their king for a new life in Opportunityland. It was a long and frightful journey, with storms and rough seas shaking their little ship and making people sick. They were often afraid, and some spoke of turning around, of giving up their dreams of a new life in this new place. Finally, a sailor high up on the mainmast shouted, "Land Ho!" and they found themselves in a beautiful new country. It felt good to put their feet on firm, dry ground after so many months at sea.

There were mountains and trees and fresh, clear streams, and in the forests they found birds, and deer, and turkeys, and lots of other animals. It was indeed a beautiful place to make a new life. There were also strange looking local people who did not speak the Islander language, but for a time they would prove to be good friends. It was not an easy life for these people in Opportunityland. The weather was cold in the winter, and food was hard to find. Many people, weak from not eating enough, became sick and died. Lucky for the rest of the Freedomlovers, their captain was a good leader and a strong man.

Captain Johnson told the Freedomlovers that they all must work together to build their homes, feed their families, and survive the long, cold winter. The captain made a strict rule that if a Freedomlover wanted to share the food gathered by the others and share the buildings they all built together, that Freedomlover must work. The wise captain knew that some people would cut wood to build the cabins and for firewood, some would sew clothing, others would look after children, and some would find food for everyone to eat. He knew that if they all did their fair share of the work, they would all have enough to eat and would survive the bitterly cold winter together.

He also knew that if some were allowed to be lazy, and their laziness was rewarded with food, he would soon have a lot of lazy people on his hands. The more people who didn't work, the more the working people would wonder why they should bother. Fewer and fewer people would work, until the working people couldn't support all the non-workers. The whole community of Freedomlovers might die because they didn't each produce their share.

This one brave man made the rules in this colony of Freedomlovers, and he did so to help the people survive. He was not mean or heartless, but he was strict because he knew all the people would die if some people took the food but didn't give anything back to the community. The Captain was fortunate that he was leader of a group of brave people who were not afraid to work for the good of themselves and their neighbors.

This one small colony of Freedomlovers did survive that first winter, thanks to the strong leadership of Captain Johnson and some help from the strange local people. The local people couldn't talk to the Freedomlovers, but they could see the Freedomlovers were hungry so they shared their food.

The next spring and summer, the locals taught the Freedomlovers how to grow corn and other food and save it for winter. In the fall, after a successful summer of farming, the Freedomlovers wanted to give thanks to their god and to their new friends. They invited the locals to a big feast of turkey, venison, pumpkin, corn, and other delicious foods.

During this meal, the Freedomlovers thanked god and they thanked their new friends for all their help. Everyone had such a good time that they agreed to do it again the next year, and this became a tradition known as "Thanklocals Day."

When the king and his banker friends heard how well the Freedomlovers were doing and how rich the land they had found was, he decided to make this new place part of the Island Kingdom. The Freedomlovers didn't mind too much because they could still worship their own god and pretty much do what they wanted with their lives. They had been born Islanders, after all, and it made them feel a little safer having a country again.

And just in case they forgot that Opportunityland belonged to the king, he sent a whole bunch of soldiers to remind them...

After a while, the king started forcing the Freedomlovers to buy things from his banker friends and to pay tax on things they bought, like coffee and tea. This started to bother the Freedomlovers because they had left the Island Kingdom to get away from the king, his control, his bankers, and his taxes. Soon the Freedomlovers realized that all the bad things they tried to leave behind in the old country had followed them to Opportunityland.

Some of the Freedomlovers started talking about fighting the king's army and making their own country with their own laws. This made the king very angry and afraid. He did not want to lose his new colony and all the riches there. The king's soldiers started taking the Freedomlovers' weapons away from them so they wouldn't be able to fight. The king's soldiers also started sleeping in the Freedomlovers' homes without being invited.

The Freedomlovers had come to Opportunityland by themselves with no help from the king and no army to protect them. They had spent their own savings on the voyage, not knowing if there would be dangerous animals or hostile people in the new

land. They had come prepared to protect themselves. They used their guns to hunt animals for food and to protect themselves from bad people. Taking a gun from a Freedomlover threatened his survival and that of his family, but the king didn't care about that. He only cared that the colonies could make him richer and more powerful.

Finally, all the rules and taxes and soldiers became too much for the Freedomlovers to accept. They went to war with the king's army and announced to the whole world that they were not part of the Island Kingdom anymore. They made their own country, and they called it "Freedomland." The king ordered his army to fight and kill all the Freedomlovers if necessary to keep Opportunityland a part of the Island Kingdom. It was a very long and bitter fight. Many people died on both sides. The soldiers burned houses and farms and killed many Freedomlovers, but the Freedomlovers never gave up. At long last, the king's general knew he and his army had been beaten, so he gave up, gathered what was left of his army, and went home.

During the war, the Freedomland government did not have enough money. At that time, most money was in the form of coins made of silver or gold, and the Freedomlovers just didn't have enough to pay for the war. Instead of letting the Freedomlovers lose the war because they didn't have enough money, a bank helped the government make paper money, and the government promised to trade the paper money for silver and gold after the war. With so much more of this paper money in the economy, and without any more things to buy, the price of everything naturally went up.

This effect, which they called *inflation*, came about because of a principle known as the law of supply and demand. Actually, the *cost* of things didn't go up. The amount of chicken food and work needed to produce one egg hasn't changed since man started raising chickens. What did go up was the *price*, which is another way of saying the value of the money went down. This is known as *inflation* because the supply of money is increased, or inflated, without actually increasing the value of the money. For example: If a dollar will buy a dozen eggs and we double the amount of dollars in circulation, soon it will take two dollars to buy a dozen eggs. The effort and chicken feed required to produce them won't have changed, but since the money supply doubled, the value of each dollar is cut in half.

The people had such a hard time with the

rising prices of food and other supplies, and it took so long for the young government to get enough gold to pay all the people for their paper money, that they decided this kind of money was no good. The pain of this economic trouble fresh in their minds, the Freedomlovers vowed never to allow this kind of "fake money" in Freedomland again. They had learned the hard lesson that if money doesn't have real value, it can ruin the economy and make it easy for bankers to take advantage of the people.

When the war was finished, the leaders of this young nation had to sit down and decide how the government would work. Would they have a king? How would they make laws, and how would they enforce them? Well, they knew they didn't want a king anymore, so they came up with a system where all the people get to choose who will fill the most important positions in government. Also, with bad memories of the money problems during the war, they made a strict rule that only their legislature could make coins and control their value. They never wanted to put a banker in charge of the money again!

Also, they wanted everyone to know that all Freedomlovers were equal, and there would be no special titles like Duke So-and-So or Count Fancypants, which the king was so fond of handing out. They even wrote down a list of rights that each Freedomlover was guaranteed. They remembered all the things the king didn't want them to do, so they made a list of rights that guaranteed each Freedomlover could do all those things.

This list promised that all Freedomlovers could have their own ideas and speak them if they wished, that the government could not take their property from them without a good reason *and* an order from a judge, that they could worship any god they chose, and that all Freedomlovers were allowed to have guns and the government could never take them away.

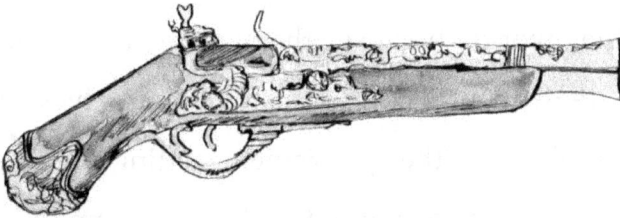

The Freedomlovers wanted everyone to understand that the Freedomland government did not *give* these rights to the people.

Freedomlovers believed that these rights were given to them—and to all people—by the god who created them. The purpose of the list of rights was only to remind people that they had them, and to tell bad people that the government would protect them as the most important rights of all. Also, the list was made to remind the government that its power came from the people. The people were the boss of the government, not the other way around like it was with the king.

The young nation grew strong and its people prospered. They were admired all over the world because they were brave and independent. They took care of themselves and didn't want the government getting involved in their lives, but when people from other lands were in trouble because of an earthquake or flood, the Freedomlovers were always first in line to send food, medical supplies, and other help. They became known around the world as hardworking, successful, and very generous people. Freedomland became a model for other countries making new governments. Freedomland was truly "opportunityland" because anyone willing to work could make a good life and earn a good living.

Freedomland became rich and the Island Kingdom became poor, so the king made a plan to take most of the money from Freedomland and give it to the Island Kingdom and its rich bankers. The king would see that all Freedomlovers would eventually work for him without actually knowing it. All the bankers in the world know each other and work together, so it was easy for the king to send some bankers to Freedomland and work out an arrangement where the rich bankers in Freedomland and the rich bankers in the Island

Kingdom would get even richer by taking money from the hardworking Freedomlovers.

Now, the Freedomlovers would never just give their money to the king, so it had to be a really sneaky plan. The Islanders talked to some bankers and some bad people in the Freedomland government, and they made their plan. They would use their power to ruin the economy in Freedomland so the people would suffer. This would help them get a new law passed giving the foreign and Freedomlover bankers the right to print all the money they wanted. They had to make a big new bank, but they couldn't call it a *bank* because Freedomlovers hated banks and bankers.

They decided to call this new bank the Freedomlovers National Safety Net, or FNSN. They would pretend that the FNSN was actually part of the government so the people would feel safe from the hated bankers. But really, it was just a big bank, run by the bankers and for the bankers.

The Islander bankers introduced their friend, an expert banker from another country. His name was Mr. Battleburg. Mr. Battleburg explained that they would help some friends of his in the Freedomland government write a new law that gave them the right to create money. The banks would be able to just print as much money as they wanted and then loan it to the people and the government. The law would also require the Freedomland government to borrow all its money from the new bank. Since the people already hated bankers, they would have to be careful not to let anyone know there were bankers involved, or that the new law would actually form a special kind of really big, really powerful bank. That's why they called it the Freedomlover's

National Safety Net, instead of the "Central Bank of Freedomland," so the ordinary people — and even most of the people in the government — would be fooled.

So Mr. Battleburg wrote the new law, and his friends in the legislature brought it to a vote one day right after most of the members had gone home for Christmas. They did not invite or even accept much discussion or debate about the new law; they just forced a vote, and the new law passed. The only legislator brave enough to speak out against this new law was a gentleman from the North Country. His name was Augustus L. Charles. Mr. Charles could see what the bankers were trying to do, so he spoke out against the new law. He argued against it in the legislature and he spoke out in public because he knew Mr. Battleburg, the king's banker, and the other bankers were just trying to steal all the Freedomlovers money. But Mr. Charles was only one man, fighting against many powerful men, so he lost.

And then Mr. Charles' beautiful farmhouse in the North Country was burned down by arsonists...

After the new law was passed to form the FNSN, the only way for money to go into circulation, to be available for people to earn, was if someone borrowed it. When you borrow money, you have to pay *interest* — which is kind of like paying to rent someone else's money. So if you borrow $100 for a year at ten percent interest, at the end of the year you have to pay the bank $110. You pay the bank the extra $10 for letting you use its money for a year. Pretty good deal, huh? If I want to loan you $100, I have to actually *have* $100. The bank just has to print it on their printing machine!

The big problem with this system is that if the only way for money to come into existence is for someone to borrow it, then there is never enough money to pay the bank back. Huh? How could that be, you ask?

It works something like this: Say you had an island with five farms on it and you decided to give those farms to five different people who would live there forever. The only rule is that you get to be the banker and print all the money. So before these five new farmers can buy tools or even eggs from each other, they need to get some money from you. You agree to loan each farmer $100 for one year at ten percent interest. That means that in one year, each farmer will have to pay you $110. They promise that they will pay you the $110 or give you their farm.

Let's see how this would work: You loan $100 to each farmer, so there is a total of $500 circulating in our little "economy." The farmers grow their crops and their animals and buy and sell to each other for a year. The day comes they must all pay you your $110. The first farmer pays you $110 and thanks you for the loan. Since you, the banker, now have $110 of the original $500 that was in circulation, there is now only $390 left in circulation. The second farmer pays you $110 and thanks you for the loan. There is now $280 left in circulation. The third farmer pays you $110 and thanks you for the loan. Now there is $170 left in circulation. The fourth farmer pays you the $110 he owes you, leaving $60 in circulation.

The last farmer approaches you with a long face. Farmer number five says that he doesn't have enough money to pay you back.

He explains he had a hard year and even though his friends, the other four farmers, loaned him all the money they had to help him pay, he still only has $60. You make a sympathetic face, but you smile inside because you know that there never was enough money for him to pay. You tell him you're sorry but remind him of your agreement.

At this point you, the banker, have a choice. You have the right to take his farm away from him right then and there. Because you're a smart banker, though, you offer the fifth farmer another loan. People work a lot harder if they think they own the farm. Of course he has to borrow enough to pay off the old loan, plus some extra to live on. It gives him a chance to keep his farm, so naturally he takes it. The other farmers also have to borrow some money so they can operate their businesses and live their lives as well—

remember, when they paid back their loans, all the money in our little economy went back into the bank. And again, the money they borrow is never enough to pay back all the loans plus interest, so at least one of them will have the same problem next year as farmer number five did this year.

You, the banker, will probably just keep loaning money back to them so you can keep them working for you on their farms, earning the money to pay you interest. But whenever you want, you can just reduce the money supply — by not loaning out any more — so the loans can't be repaid and you can start taking their farms away from them.

See why it's so dangerous to put bankers in charge of the money?

Now, back to our story...

So the king's government was in a lot of trouble. They didn't have enough gold to pay for all things the king wanted to buy. The Island's products were expensive, and Freedomland's products were lower priced, so none of the Freedomlovers wanted to buy the Islander's products even though they had enough money to do so. The bankers knew that the Freedomlovers would never start buying Island products just to help the Islanders, so they had to think of a way to get them to send their money to the Island Kingdom voluntarily.

The bankers in Freedomland started loaning out a lot of money. Since they had the right to just print however much they wanted, they simply printed it out and loaned it to anyone who asked. Since there was a lot of money floating around in the economy, people bought a lot of things, so more workers were needed, so wages went up, so the workers needed to buy more things, so more factories were built, and so on. This also made the price of products go up, which didn't seem so important at the time, but it did make the Island products more affordable in comparison.

It seemed like a great time! The people were making money, and a lot of them were getting rich. Then prices went so high that

Island products were cheaper than Freedomlover products, so a lot of Freedomlover money went to the Island to buy things like clothes, furniture, and other stuff. We all want to buy lower priced things, don't we? Well, the Freedomland economy was still growing like crazy, and people were still buying things, and borrowing money, and buying stock, and feeling richer and richer all the time.

But then the day came when even the bankers couldn't keep up with all the money leaving to go to the Island Kingdom, and there just wasn't enough money left in Freedomland to run the country. People tried to take their money out of their banks, but the banks didn't have it to give them because it had all already gone to the Island Kingdom. There was a huge panic, and lots of banks had to close because they had no money. Factories closed, people lost their jobs, stocks lost their value, and most people lost all their money.

Another problem for the bankers was that they had promised to trade all the dollars they issued for gold—but they had issued more dollars than they had gold! So if everyone took their dollars to the bank and demanded gold, the banks wouldn't have nearly enough gold to go around. So the president, Mr. Rosey Delayno, told the people that anyone who had gold in their home was causing the problems with the economy. He issued an order that everyone had to turn in their gold to the government in exchange for paper money, and that paper money couldn't be traded for gold anymore. The people knew that their money had no more real value anymore, so they lost even more confidence in the economy.

Many had borrowed money to buy houses and farms and now had no way to earn the money to pay the bank. When the so-called experts at the FNSN were asked what the problem was, they stroked their chins, looked thoughtful, and said augustly, "Oh, the economy is hard to predict. It's bad now, though. There just isn't enough money! These are bad times. We'll all just have to do our best."

At the same time, the banks started taking homes and farms from people who couldn't make their payments. They pretended they were sorry about it so the people wouldn't feel bad, but how can you not feel bad when someone takes your house away?

For over ten years, the economic doldrums stayed with the Freedomlovers. Many, many people lost their homes and their farms, and all the experts at the banks would say was, "These are bad times. We all have to do our best. There just isn't enough money!"

Then something terrible happened. A World War! The Freedomlovers had to help the Islanders protect their country from the Battleburgers. The Battleburgers wanted to take over the world and make everyone who wasn't a Battleburger into a slave. The Islanders and their powerful friends in the Freedomland government convinced the Freedomlovers that if the Island Kingdom was conquered by the Battleburgers, then Freedomland wouldn't be far behind. The Freedomlovers still didn't want to be slaves, so they knew they had to fight.

But wait a minute, you say! The Freedomland government didn't have any money! How could they buy guns and planes and tanks and bullets and all the other things you need for a war—like bandages and hospital beds—when they had no money? Their good friends the bankers, led by Mr. Battleburg and his friends, loaned them all the money they needed! Wasn't that kind of the bankers? A bit odd though, wouldn't you say? Mr. Battleburg loaning money to the Freedomlovers to help the Islanders fight the Battleburgers?

And boy, did the Freedomland government borrow money from the FNSN bankers! Can you imagine the trillions of dollars the Freedomland Government needed to put 10,000,000 soldiers, sailors, and marines in uniform and equip them with weapons, ships, and tanks, and then to feed them and take care of them when they were sick and wounded? And to pay life insurance to their families when they were killed in battle? The number has so many zeros you can hardly count them all!

But our good friends, the bankers, were happy to loan the Freedomlovers all the money they needed to fight the terrible Battleburgers. After all, the Freedomlovers were fighting for their lives, for their very freedom! The bankers also didn't mind collecting the interest on loans they made with money they just printed on their printing machine. Pretty good deal for the bankers, wouldn't you say? Most of us have to actually earn the money before we can loan it to someone else, but a bank can just create it out of nothing!

When the government started buying lots of things for the war, the factories opened up, and people went back to work and started earning money. They could buy food for their children and themselves, so although they were sad and afraid about the war, they were happy to have jobs.

Well, the Freedomlovers went off and

fought the Battleburgers and beat them. It took four years, but they did it and boy, were they proud! Since everyone had been working during the war, many people could get loans to buy back their old houses. Everyone was so happy about winning the war, having jobs, and being back in their own houses again that they didn't realize what the bankers had done to them…

…Aren't you wondering how it was that for over ten years, the FNSN banks had no money to lend the people, but suddenly, when there was a war, there was no limit to the amount of money they could loan to the government?

The Freedomlovers were so happy that the war was over, and that there was work for everyone, that almost none of them wondered about how their supply of money went from almost nothing to nearly unlimited in just a matter of months.

But there were a few...

These few began to wonder if the cryptic prophecy of one of the Founding Fathers of Freedomland, Mr. Jeff Thomason, hadn't already come true. This sage, a beloved statesman and third president of Freedomland, had told his young nation:

> I believe that banks are more dangerous to our liberties than standing armies. If the Freedomlovers ever allow private banks to control the creation of money, first by inflation, then by deflation, the banks will deprive the people of all property until their children wake up homeless on the continent their fathers conquered. The

power to create money should remain with
the people, to whom it properly belongs.

Some of the Freedomlovers began to understand that when the banks can create money out of nothing, they can create a whole lot of it by lending it out freely. They know that people will borrow money to build houses and factories and other things they need, but whenever the bank wants, it can just stop lending money.

When the bank stops lending money and people keep making their loan payments, the amount of money in the economy gradually gets smaller and smaller. Sooner or later, there will simply not be enough money out there for people to continue to make those loan payments, no matter how hard they work. Then the banks start taking away houses again.

The people who understand this are frustrated. When they try to explain it, their friends don't listen and say things like, "Money is money. It's like air or water. I just don't have enough of it." These savvy citizens want to shout from the rooftops that there is a limited amount of water on this planet, and a limited amount of air, but THERE IS NO LIMIT TO THE AMOUNT OF MONEY A BANK CAN CREATE FROM NOTHING. THIS IS HOW THEY CHEAT US OUT OF OUR WORK!

They try and try, but so few people listen. And so they wonder:

Will the Freedomlovers ever learn?

Thank You

Thank you for *reading Once Upon a Time, A Financial Fable*. If you liked this book, I'm sure you'll enjoy *Honest Money*.

If you will kindly sign up for The Daily Diatribe Newsletter, I'll send you a link to download the eBook version for free!

Join the Freedomlovers!
http://www.dailydiatribe.net

You have my word I will never sell or share your e-mail address, nor will I bombard you with annoying advertisements. Of course, you can easily and conveniently unsubscribe any time by simply clicking on the "unsubscribe" button, which will be present in every newsletter.

For news about upcoming books, such as *When All Else Fails*, about how failing to follow the Constitution has caused most of the problems in the USA, and *Sex, Lies, & Carbohydrates, How I accidentally lost 30 Pounds*, you can also visit my website at:

http://www.dailydiatribe.net

Or the Daily Diatribe Facebook page at:

http://www.facebook.com/dailydiatribe

Thanks for reading!

Warm regards,

Carl

www.ingramcontent.com/pod-product-compliance
Lightning Source LLC
Chambersburg PA
CBHW070947210326
41520CB00021B/7096